PRAISE FOR PROHIBITION WINE

"As a feminist and aging activist, I found *Prohibition Wine* compelling. This book highlights the importance of giving voice to women's stories as part of American history. It is relevant today as current generations of immigrant women rise up to the challenges of life. It touches the lives of all of us across multiple generations as we all cope with the pandemic challenges. *Prohibition Wine* is powerful narrative and inspiring read!"

—JOAN DITZION, LICSW, co-founder of Our Bodies Ourselves and co-author of all nine editions of *Our Bodies, Ourselves; Ourselves And Our Children*; and *Our Bodies, Ourselves: Menopause*

"We first meet a feisty teenaged Rebecca Goldberg fleeing a Cossack and later as a young widow who became a bootlegger. Hats off to Marian Knapp for uncovering this power-

...ful story of her grandmother and sharing it with us!"

—**Pamela S. Nadell**, author, Director of the Jewish Studies Program and Patrick Clendenen Chair in Women's & Gender History at American University

"Marian Knapp's reconstruction of Rebecca Goldberg's life as a Jewish immigrant, a struggling widow and mother, and a Prohibition-era bootlegger both confirms and confounds our preconceived notions of the history of American Jewish women. This little book goes deep into the archives, telling a story that heightens our understanding of the past and our empathy for those who lived through it."

—**Marni Davis**, author of *Jews and Booze* and Associate Professor, Georgia State University

℘ROHIBITIOꞶ WINE

A True Story of One Woman's
Daring in Twentieth-Century America

MARIAN LEAH KNAPP

SHE WRITES PRESS

Published 2021
Printed in the United States of America
Print ISBN: 978-1-64742-061-1
E-ISBN: 978-1-64742-062-8
Library of Congress Control Number: 2020917551

For information, address:
She Writes Press
1569 Solano Ave #546
Berkeley, CA 94707

Cover and interior design by Tabitha Lahr

She Writes Press is a division of SparkPoint Studio, LLC.

In memory of

LOUIS GILBERT
who became "the man" of
the family at age fourteen.

LENA GOLDBERG BOBROW
who secretly carried pints of
illegal booze to local officials.

EDWARD GOLDBERG
who searched the roadsides and
dump for pocket-size bottles.

CONTENTS

Author's Note

Rebecca Wernick Goldberg was my grandmother. I met her only once, but don't remember because I was too young. She died when I was eighteen months old before any real-life happenings had fixed themselves in my memory. Even though I have no concrete image of Rebecca to carry with me, her presence was very much a part of my growing up.

For many years, when my father Lou, my aunt Lena, and uncles Eddie and Joe gathered, I listened to their stories about their childhoods and what they and their mother did to survive daunting, dismal circumstances. Lou and Eddie wrote soulful stream-of-consciousness autobiographies with an aura of disbelief on how they managed to get through it all. Lou focused on how he overcame traumatic events and ultimately conquered formidable barriers. Eddie wrote about lacking a father to guide him through his early life. Lena told me stories about her siblings and intimate details about Rebecca that her sons never knew. My aunts Bessie and Minnie had died in young adulthood, before I could know them, appreciate them, and hear their own personal narratives.

Throughout the first decades of my life, I knew that someday I would tell the Goldberg story, thinking it would focus on my dad, aunts, and uncles and their individual struggles to establish successful lives, but I could never quite determine how to do this. They had already documented their own histories, and I became wary of trying to edit their thoughts and feelings. Then, one morning I awoke with the intense realization that rather than write about Rebecca's children, I had to write about her. My job then became to unravel, understand, and tell her story. Although her children had hard lives, she was the one who created the foundation from which they could step out into the future and have a more promising, less uncertain existence than her own.

With my decision to bring Rebecca into the forefront, I began a journey of learning. I started by reading and rereading the two autobiographies and listening to recordings of Lena's recollections. I found that out of hundreds of typewritten pages and extensive interviews, only a handful of comments about their mother emerged. What was said about her was mostly brief remarks with little detail, such as "she came from Vilna," "she slapped an aggressive Cossack in a tavern and ran home in the snow without shoes," or "her sister Leah died in Gloversville, New York, when an oil lamp fell on her at the end of a day making gloves."

Each written or oral statement about Rebecca led me to streams of questions: What was she doing in a tavern? Why did she and her family leave Vilna for America? What overland route did she take from Vilna to a port of departure? Whom did she travel with? What ship did she take? Why did she end up in Boston? Ultimately, what drew her into the sale of illegal alcohol?

Each question sent me on a series of poignant explorations. By the time I set out on my search, none of the older generation were alive for me to ask them questions. What I did have, in addition to the autobiographies, interviews, and hand-me-down tales, were a few family photographs, old newspaper articles, and headlines.

I searched Ancestry.com for immigration records; retrieved city directories, census, and death data for Boston and other cities starting from the late 1880s; and accessed archives from Yeshiva University in New York. I read many books and articles on the status of immigrant women; family life among religious Jewish settlers; health, illness, and common life-threatening accidents in the late nineteenth and early twentieth centuries; and what health services were available for prevention and treatment. How people got around in those eras and the importance and prevalence of trains emerged as important topics. All of these elements were part of the immigrant life.

But the most significant moment for Rebecca was when she decided to enter into the illegal alcohol trade during Prohibition. The history leading up to the Volstead Act and ultimate Prohibition, its advocates and opponents, what was restricted and what was permitted was a major part of my information gathering. I learned about the enactment of Prohibition, its enforcement, and how illegal alcohol was produced and distributed, and the attempts at getting around the law.

Some of my most powerful experiences came when I tried to find locations where Rebecca lived, worked, or passed through. I walked the oldest Jewish cemeteries in Dedham, Massachusetts, hoping to find Rebecca's sister Leah's grave, but all I came up with were headstones covered in ancient moss, facedown in the dirt, pitted by years of weather or simply labeled with "unknown." I walked from Boston's North End following the path Rebecca and her sisters took on the way to a glove factory in the South End and imagined what it was like plodding through the mess as the first Boston subway route was being built.

Each time I found a new newspaper headline or bit of historical data, it helped broaden my understanding of Rebecca's life and the environment in which she lived. Each scrap of material provided a clue to the quality of her life, personality, and perseverance.

I had already known where Rebecca, her husband Nathan, and her children were buried, and had visited their graves from time to time. I left stones on their headstones. Because of my investigations, now, when I go to the cemeteries, I have a far greater depth of awareness about what this family went through, and what Rebecca did to launch her children into a world so much more stable and hopeful than her own. I am filled with esteem for her courage.

Once in a while I wonder how Rebecca would react to my writing her life story. Having learned a bit about how she viewed her life, I think she would be annoyed with me. She would say it was none of my business, that I was butting into her private life, or that she was only doing what she had to do. Just as she never wanted a fancy dress, she wouldn't be able to accept my admiration and respect. She lived her life sticking to the basics—working hard, finding ways to put food on the table, and enduring tragedies. Most of all she was clear and remained steadfast in the goals she set for herself and her children—stay together, survive, and get an education. She never deviated from this vision by plodding ahead one arduous step at a time.

INTRODUCTION

In a many ways Rebecca Goldberg wasn't unusual. She was the same as millions of others who, in the late nineteenth and early twentieth centuries, fled the oppressive Russian Empire in the hope of finding a safe and stable place to live. She yearned to be free of threatening anti-Semitism and, most importantly, have the chance for a future that was more hopeful than what was possible for her and her family in Vilna, Lithuania. Even in America, she knew that because she was a woman and illiterate, she had few options but to learn a trade, help support her family, marry in the prescribed order from oldest to youngest daughters, and wed a man she may not be able to choose for herself. She bore children with no way to decide how many, and she watched some of them die. None of this was unique for that era.

Yet, her determination to survive, and, maybe even thrive, was powerful. Rebecca had the stubborn, innate force to find solutions to the daunting problems she faced and to keep moving forward. Her life was comprised of sadness, smattered with pleasure, but mostly it reflected a woman of dogged perseverance and strong will.

She journeyed through significant historical periods that had major impacts on the grand and complex landscape around her, but in which she was a barely noticeable participant. In photographs of masses of steerage passengers arriving at US entry ports, she is one of those peering out in expectation and wonder, but no one now would be able to recognize her or know her name.

In America, she was anonymous in the crowds of people who walked the teeming streets of Boston's North End on her way to work. She was among the vast numbers who woke to a daily grind of earning enough to buy food to keep family members nourished while maintaining the vision of a life that would be better for herself and those she cared about.

She was known within her family, of course, but once she stepped outside that protective milieu, she was just another figure in a world that offered a positive vision, but which also set up barriers to achieving that dream. Rebecca did survive and ultimately achieved important personal goals that were wondrous, but not without suffering. This is her story.

Chapter I

GETTING TO AMERICA

In the winter of 1886, Simon Wernick and his teenage daughter, Rebecca, stopped at a tavern during a peddling trek around Vilna Guberniya, one of the many governmental subdivisions in the vast Russian Empire. He made his circuit with a horse and a buggy that held his wares along with anyone who was traveling with him. Rebecca's three older sisters, Betsy, Leah, and Gitel, were not with them on that day. In the Pale of Settlement, which was the defined, restricted area in which Jews were allowed to live, it was not unusual for merchants like Simon to bring their children or wives with them on sales rounds in the countryside.

A tavern was a logical and fairly protected place for this father and daughter to stop because the proprietor would have been someone like himself, a Jew. There were many places along his route where he could have found some welcome because, at this time, almost sixty percent of all taverns in the Pale were owned or overseen by Jews. These taverns served people living in these communities including wealthy aristocratic landowners, poor peasants, soldiers, Cossacks, and Jews.

Cabaret Jews (Tselovalniki?)
Jankiel in Adam Mickiewicz's epic poem, Pan Tadeusz
Courtesy of the Esther M. Zimmer Lederberg
Memorial Website http://www.estherlederberg.com/home.html

The Cossacks were fierce mercenaries who were loyal to the Tsar and his local administrators, and who were generally feared. During this era, Cossacks were charged with carrying out the Tsar's orders, which included keeping the peace while periodically instigating peasants to perpetrate violence against Jews. There was good reason to be afraid and wary. Any misstep could end in retribution on an individual or a whole village.

On this winter day, among the roadhouse patrons were a number of Cossacks. Everyone recognized them, knew their reputation, and kept their distance. It was bitterly cold outside, and Rebecca sat near the stove to warm herself. She was a handsome, strong-looking girl with no shoes. Maybe she had taken off her shoes to thaw her icy feet, or maybe she didn't have any shoes at all.

One of the Cossacks noticed her and his powerful status gave him the right to approach without asking permission. He broke away from his compatriots and lunged aggressively towards Rebecca. When he began to touch her, she instinctively tried to stop his advances and slapped his face hard. Terrified at what she had done, she fled out the door without her father and without shoes. She ran barefoot for miles in the snow to her familiar shtetl and hid behind the house's stove—the *pripetchik*—using it, naively, as protection. If the Cossack had decided to pursue her, the house and oven would have offered no shelter. Simon followed in panic, not knowing where she had gone, but was greatly relieved when he found her safe at home. No one had followed her.

The Wernicks' living arrangement was similar to that of tens of thousands of poor Jews. Shtetls were small, self-contained settlements with at least one shul (synagogue), a marketplace, tradespeople, and hundreds of residents living in fragile harmony with hostile neighbors, maintaining a Jewish life, and feeding their families in an ever-present, threatening environment. Conditions were generally deplorable. Rebecca, her mother Hannah (known as Anna), her father, and seven siblings shared a tiny one-room, dirt-floored dwelling. Their livestock lived inside with them.

Other than this story of fending off the Cossack, Rebecca's early years are blurred, surrounded by vagueness and imprecision. Any details about her childhood and early teen years come from the few memories that she recounted to her children and what they later reported. Yet this one incident provides a telling clue about Rebecca's strong will, her instinctive drive for self-preservation, and her intense need to be in control of her own life.

The episode in the tavern may have been the pivotal incident that convinced Simon it was time to leave for America. He had already seen too much misery and uncertainty about the future for Jews. Anti-Semitism had always been a threat in Lithuania, as it was throughout the Russian Empire. Jews were limited in where they could live, certain occupations were closed to them, and only a few were allowed to own property. The imperial authority exploited long-embedded hatreds to encourage local populations to threaten and attack Jews. It became clear to Simon that there was no prospect for his family there. He also knew that once they left, there would be no going back. Despite the risks, uncertainties, and fear of the unknown, Simon packed a few belongings and headed towards a new beginning. He went alone with plans to bring the rest of the family to America as soon as possible.

By the time he began his journey in 1887, railroads could take travelers long distances, sparing them endless days of walking or travelling by horse and wagon. Steamships had cut Atlantic crossings to two or three weeks compared to a month or more in sailing vessels. Steamship companies had agents selling passage tickets in major cities. Still, although the Tsarist regime from time to time encouraged emigration, or at least looked the other way, it was a frightening journey to undertake. Jews and other emigrants defied the laws, often fleeing at night in order to avoid Russian border guards and roving highway gangs. They bribed officials to let them leave.

Simon, who was in his early 40s, embarked alone from Hamburg on June 12, 1887, on the steamship *Rugia* and arrived in New York on June 25. The *Rugia* made a direct crossing to New York with an inspection stop at Le Havre, France. Simon was examined and processed at Castle Garden at the tip of Manhattan, because

NORTH END
Image source and copyright unknown.

Ellis Island didn't open until April 1890. When he sailed into New York Harbor, he saw the Statue of Liberty, which had been dedicated the previous year. Simon's whereabouts for the eighteen months between his arrival in the summer of 1887 and the winter of 1889, or why he chose to settle in Boston, are unknown. He was probably drawn there because he knew a Vilna *landsman*—a fellow Jew from the same district—who had arrived previously and who shared his particular history and religious practice. In the 1890 Boston City directory, he is listed as a grocer at two addresses: 81 Prince Street and 158 Salem Street in the North End.

In the North End there were Lithuanian and Russian shuls, some traditional and others more progressive. Several Lithuanian shuls had founders and members from Vilna. In 1889, about twelve shuls or minyans (a religious group of at least ten men) were close to Prince and Salem Streets. Simon would have wanted to live and work within walking distance of a very traditional house of worship. He was a biblical scholar with passionate and rigid views on what it meant to be a Jew. He wanted to be in a community of like-minded men.

At this time, Boston's North End was a tightly packed neighborhood filled with immigrants that started arriving in different ethnic waves in the early to mid-nineteenth century. The Irish had arrived in the 1840s to escape the great potato famine. They were largely unskilled laborers working on the railroads, in maintenance and construction, or as domestic help. Jews began to arrive in the mid-nineteenth century and made a living in skilled work such as tailoring and garment manufacturing. Many were peddlers or operated small shops. Italians started coming in the 1860s and mostly worked in commercial fishing, shipping, and later in subway construction, and they too were peddlers and shopkeepers, selling goods that reflected their old-world culture. With the massive late nineteenth century influx from Eastern Europe and the Russian Empire, almost one-third of the North End's population was Jewish.

Once Simon had found a place to live and a way to earn a living, he began to send money to his family in Russia so that they could emigrate. His oldest daughter, Betsy, came next to join her father and look after his personal and household needs. The three next oldest daughters came together a year or so later: Leah (Lea), age eighteen; Kate (Gitel), age sixteen; and Rebecca (Rivke), age fourteen. Passenger lists gave approximate ages and census data is unreliable, so these ages may not be exact. Other records suggest that Rebecca was a bit older than what had been recorded at her arrival in America.

To get to America, the sisters made their way to Hamburg, Germany. Their route was likely from Vilna to Kibarty, Lithuania, to the German border crossing at Eydtkuhnen, roughly 125 miles from Vilna. If the sisters had taken the steam locomotive train to the German border, the journey could have been as little as four to five hours. If they walked, it would have been many days. Eydtkuhnen is where many escaping Jews crossed over, leaving Tsarist Russia forever. It was the largest border town where the German government had established a control station. Here immigrants were examined for potential health conditions before beginning their seven-hundred-mile trek to Hamburg. Well before the sisters arrived at the border, a small number of Jews had decided to stay in Eydtkuhnen and offer help to those who were traveling through on their way to America. They provided food, shelter, and familiar conversation.

Once the sisters passed their physical examinations, they crossed the border and walked or traveled by train or cart to the port at Hamburg. Throughout their travels, there was the threat of assault, hunger, robbery, injury, and even death. The young women were helped by networks of friends or family members with connections to their Vilna community. They carried very little with them: some food, maybe a change or two of clothing, and a blanket. They slept in a pigsty at least once. In total, they journeyed close to nine hundred miles over many weeks to get to Hamburg where they would board a ship for the new world. Although they were just a tiny trio of emigrants clinging to each other for comfort and safety, they were surrounded by a vast forward-moving wave of people with the same driven desire to be free and determined to create new lives.

Merging with the flow on June 18, 1889, the three sisters boarded the ship *Prague* which deposited them in Glasgow, Scotland. At Glasgow they embarked on the *Furnesia* to New York, where they arrived on July 6, 1889. Then they took the train to Boston to join Simon.

Chapter II

EARLY IN AMERICA

———— ❈ ————

On December 23, 1889, less than six months after the three sisters had arrived, Simon, dressed in the black, ankle-length attire of a religious Jew, stood at an open grave at a cemetery in Dedham, Massachusetts. If it hadn't been for his flaming-red hair and beard, he would have looked like any other Jewish traditionalist in immigrant-laden Boston.

He was there to bury Leah, his second-oldest daughter. Shortly after the sisters had landed in Boston, they traveled by train to Gloversville, New York. Extensive train routes in the northeast region connected small towns with bigger cities and allowed for the transportation of goods, travelers, and workers. All four teenage girls went to learn how to stitch gloves and be trained as skilled laborers, which offered opportunities for better paying jobs. On subsequent marriage and census records, the surviving sisters indicated their occupations as either glove makers or seamstresses. They had all followed the same course. Clues about why they went to Gloversville are sparse, but the Helpern family, originally from Vilna, had helped Wernick family members over many years by finding them jobs in the tradition of one compatriot helping another. Solomon Helpern who came here with training as a tanner made his way to Gloversville in the late 1880s because it was a well-known glove manufacturing center in the country. Later, at the turn of the century, Helpern came back to Boston and opened his own shop in Boston's South End.

The promising training in Gloversville and the opportunity for work ended in tragedy for the Wernicks. Within only a few months of their arrival in Gloversville, Leah was dead. The sisters were working in a factory or one of the numerous small sweatshops in homes or tenements. It was the end of the day, December 21, 1889, when one of the sisters reached up to turn off the oil lamps that lit the dark interior. One of the lamps fell on Leah, whose clothing caught fire, and the three watched in horror as she was quickly enveloped in flames. Fires like this were not uncommon during this era when unprotected fire was used to provide light, heat, and for cooking. Also, in that era women wore voluminous, flammable clothing. Safety measures were lax or nonexistent, and there were few ways to put fires out quickly. Even if there had been immediate help for Leah, once her dress ignited, she would have been instantly engulfed in flames. Reports of accidental deaths by fire were routine in local newspapers.

How Leah, either dead or barely alive, got back to Boston is unknown, but it was likely by train as they had arrived. Her death record from Massachusetts Hospital, which names her parents, says "accident, burns, thirty-six hours, burial Dedham," but no documentation of Leah's grave site exists. If Rebecca knew where it was, she never revealed the location. Perhaps she didn't know. Jewish tradition prohibits traditional burial if a body is damaged in some way, as it would have been with burns. However, Jewish tradition also says that since Leah's death was an accident, she still would have been entitled to a religious burial. But, because of her body's condition, the Jewish burial society may not have been able to perform the prescribed ritual cleansing and Simon's ultra-conservative interpretations may have prevailed. For whatever unknown reasons, knowledge of Leah's tomb has been lost.

From his earliest days in the United States, Simon was known by the nickname "Big Red." When people called him that, it was not with gentle familiarity, but with aversion and fear. He was demanding and overbearing, ruling over his family with a power that no one dared to challenge. If his wife or any one of his children contradicted him, they were subjected to ridicule for not living up to his standard. This attribute pervaded all aspects of their existence, particularly their religious lives. In addition to Simon's domineering fundamentalist nature, it was a time when women were often devalued, particularly in death. It was not uncommon to bury a woman with the headstone saying "Mr. Cohen's wife," "Mrs. Levine's sister," or simply "unknown."

Leah's death was the first of numerous tragic events in Rebecca's life in America, but for the next ten years her existence seemed peaceful and uneventful, with no major troublesome happenings. Extended family members lived close to each other in different Boston neighborhoods and the focus for everyone was on earning a living, sharing daily occurrences, spending social time together, and gathering for holiday observance.

Chapter III

CALM AFTER TRAGEDY

———⊰⊱———

Simon's wife Anna (Hannah) arrived in New York on July 12, 1890, with the four younger Wernick children: (Ester), age fifteen; Michael (Rachmel), age twelve; Arthur (Oser), age eight; and Morris (Moses), less than three years. After their arduous journey and when they got to Boston, Simon told them that Leah was dead. For Anna, the grief and deep disillusionment was profound. In a Russia of constant danger and threat, she and Simon had managed to protect their children. Yet here, in the promise of America, Leah had died, not by a Cossack or peasant attack, but in an unintended industrial accident. The family never talked about this loss.

It was deemed improper to discuss such events, with the belief that speaking about them would slow the healing process; better to be silent and simply move on.

Rebecca and her older sisters never returned to Gloversville, but remained in Boston close to the rest of the family. Although the family doesn't show up on the 1890 US Census, Simon's name is listed in city directories as doing business in the North End each year during the decade of the 1890s.

Simon and Anna managed a small store, which Anna ran while Simon studied Torah. Because the Wernick male children were young when they arrived here, they were able to go to school, learn to read and write, and graduate from high school. Unfortunately, Rebecca had been too old to attend school when she came to America and she remained illiterate in English for the rest of her life. Esther, like her older sisters, was also trained as a glove maker. The Wernicks followed the custom that children lived at home, bringing in money for the family until marriage. Even after a child married, it was common for her or him to live close by their parents and, if necessary, contribute financially if they could. It was through financial contributions of all immediate family members that people were able to survive. Group responsibility and not individual desires was the accepted practice.

Between 1890 and 1900 Rebecca and her sisters were employed making gloves at the Helpern-owned factory on LaGrange Street in the South End. Today, it seems as if Boston's North and South Ends are far apart, but the physical distance is less than two miles and an easy walk between the two neighborhoods. To get to her job, Rebecca walked down Salem Street, across Scollay Square, to Tremont Street, along the side of the Boston Common, which is the oldest public park in the country. She then took a left on LaGrange Street to the glove factory at number 36-46. It would have taken less than an hour depending on how long Rebecca stopped to watch what was going on around her. At the end of the nineteenth century, the streets were increasingly crowded with more and more immigrants, noisy from clanging surface trolley cars, and the smell of horse manure fouled the air.

To mitigate congestion and filth, the city of Boston with assistance from the state decided to

SUBWAY CONSTRUCTION
Image source and copyright unknown.

bury a transportation line under the street. As Rebecca and her sisters made their way to work, the first underground rail line in the country was being built under Tremont Street. With two stops, it was meant to reduce the chaos on the street between Park and Boylston Streets. Rebecca watched the construction progress for several years as she walked through mess and mud, being careful not to soil her long skirt.

The girls' income from sewing gloves and a little bit of money from the older boys who had jobs after school kept the family stable. They all worked hard during the week, strictly observed the Sabbath, celebrated Jewish holidays, and kept the Passover traditions. The Wernicks' growing community of family and friends formed a critical foundation for Rebecca that lasted through her early years, her marriage, and for the rest of her life. This familial cocoon formed a solid, reliable base. She could not have known as a young woman how essential these relationships would be for her long-term welfare and basic survival. She would never have made it through without them.

After the initial few years in America, however, this closeness became a burden for Rebecca's brothers, Michael and Arthur. They found this intimate, prescribed environment oppressive, and shortly after they each graduated from high school, they left the family fold, ultimately settling in different parts of the country. But Rebecca couldn't go off on her own. She was an uneducated woman whose destiny was to get married and stay near her parents.

Sometime after 1898, the Wernicks moved from the North End to the South End, where Simon became involved with the establishment of a new traditional congregation, Kenesseth Israel, known as the Emerald Street synagogue. He was a prominent figure in this shul, which formed a strong religious community for him.

Rebecca's older sisters had each married in the years before 1900. Now it was her turn to find a husband. Her photograph in an embroidered dress was probably taken for a matchmaker to show to potential suitors. Her hair is short in this picture—unusual in a time of bouffant coifs. Her thin, sparse hair was a permanent element of her appearance, and she was forever unhappy about it.

A husband was found for Rebecca, and she wed Nathan Goldberg, a store keeper, on January 4, 1900. It is not possible to know how much initiative or input she had in the choice.

REBECCA, age twenty-four
Family Photo

Chapter IV

NATHAN AND EARLY MARRIAGE

Family lore has it that Nissan (Nathan) Majofis "walked across Russia" from Dvinsk, Latvia, which, at times, was part of Lithuania–Poland. Nathan left his homeland in search of his father, Israel, who had emigrated to Palestine in the early 1880s. Unlike Rebecca's father, Simon, who was a scholarly Jew, Israel Majofis was a Zionist who believed his mission was to be part of a movement to reclaim the land that Jews had considered their homeland for three thousand years. Zionism was among the many social, religious, and political groups active in Eastern European Jewish society. There were Jews who were anxious to leave for places like America to be able to pursue dreams of a new life, including being able to practice their religion in their own way and without fear. There were others who hoped to stay and modernize and change the status of Jews through labor unions or "bunds." Still others eschewed traditional Jewish practice by creating new ways to interpret old laws. Some even advocated and tried to find new locations to establish Jewish colonies in places around the world, especially in South America. And then there were Zionists who saw no hope in the old world but believed that Jews could only be safe in the holy Promised Land.

So, Nathan set out to find his Zionist father. To get to Palestine, Nathan gradually made his way south, through Kiev to Odessa, a trip of about six hundred miles. He worked at small jobs to pay for his travel. At Odessa, he found passage on a boat that took him through the Turkish Straits to Smyrna (Izmir) on the Aegean Sea. From there, it was another thousand miles to Jaffa, the only major port in nineteenth-century Palestine.

After many months of grueling travel, Nathan arrived in the Holy Land. He spent some time searching for his father, but his pilgrimage ended up with profound disappointment. Israel had been murdered by local people, and Nathan ultimately found his grave.

With the hope of being united with his father shattered, Nathan decided to head to America. From Jaffa he took a ship to Liverpool, England, where he boarded the *Labrador*, arriving in Quebec on September 15, 1895. He walked across the Canadian border into the United States just a week later on September 21. Somewhere along the way he lost his original name, and Nissan Majofis became Nathan Goldberg.

The Majofis name has an interesting history. It was associated with bands of musicians who were at the beck and call of the Tsar and local governing officials to perform. They were deemed very low on the social scale because of their subservient behavior. They were totally dependent upon the charity of rulers. In Tsarist Russia, the name Majofis signified a minstrel Jew who was willing to demean himself before gentiles. Ironically and poignantly, their name stems from the lovely Old Testament words *ma yafit*, meaning *how beautiful*. It is understandable that after reaching his new country, Nathan was happy to discard the Majofis stigma.

Nathan came by himself to America. Like Rebecca, he had a big family, but in contrast to her experience, he left his family behind and set out on his own. He quickly lost contact with his brothers and sisters, and they never knew what had become of him. He was educated in Jewish tradition, but ultimately chose to abandon it, being a product of a culture that was questioning custom and seeking new solutions that would lead to a more peaceful and sustainable life.

Handed-down stories paint Nathan as a maverick—someone who didn't follow other people's rules. Nathan's life wasn't long enough for him to know that of his seven brothers and sisters who had remained in Eastern Europe, only his oldest brother, Zvi Hirsh, survived to produce a family. His other siblings and their families remained in Latvia and died in the Holocaust.

Nathan relished change, and his incessant desire to keep searching for something new was an underlying theme of his early existence. He was constantly seeking a new idea, a new way to earn a living, a new place to live. He had a compelling personality, a strong body, and a powerful but unsettled persona.

After arriving in Canada and crossing into the US, Nathan roamed, walked, and worked in various jobs before he got to Lowell, Massachusetts. By 1850, Lowell had become the second largest city in Massachusetts, the largest industrial center in the US, and a promising place for a new immigrant and ultimately a young couple to get started. Nathan must have heard about it during his journey to America.

This is who Rebecca married on January 4, 1900. She was about twenty-four, and Nathan was twenty-six. He was a progressive thinker, a challenger of tradition and exhibited a freedom of beliefs that Rebecca may have yearned for in light of her domineering father and her constricted upbringing. Still, Nathan was willing to work hard, while a more religious husband may have spent most of his time studying, thereby requiring his wife to earn a living. Nathan was also an adventurer with a confident outlook and he could show Rebecca ideas, places, and things she would not have seen otherwise. These aspects of Nathan's personality may have been attractive to Rebecca, even though she probably didn't have much choice in his selection as her husband. The marriage was likely arranged because she was next in line for marriage and she was getting close to being too old to find a mate. In their wedding picture Rebecca and Nathan look like a strong, intense couple. Their fancy clothing was rented. They would not have had the money to purchase such luxuries.

The early years of their marriage seemed tentative. In 1900 Nathan was doing business in *pictures*, in 1904 he was a collector, and in 1906 he was a tea peddler in five or six different Lowell locations.

Rebecca gave birth to four children in as many years. Bessie (registered as Pauline) was born on January 17, 1901. Twelve months later, Joey (recorded as George), was born, on January 13, 1902. Lou was born on February 20, 1904, and Minnie on August 30, 1905. Rebecca suffered another tragedy when her second child, Joey died from measles in May 1908, shortly

REBECCA AND NATHAN, wedding
Family Photo

after his sixth birthday. She never recovered from this loss and forever told her other children that none of them could compare to him.

During the years in Lowell, Rebecca and Nathan moved among various apartments, not being able to settle down or establish a stable place to live. Nathan was on the road a lot. Sometimes the whole family or just a few of the children would go with him; sometimes he went alone. He traveled with a horse and wagon between Lowell and Norwich, Connecticut, a journey of about one hundred miles. He also went to Binghamton, New York, and Scranton, Pennsylvania. Locally, he travelled in endless trips back and forth to Somerville, Cambridge, and different Boston neighborhoods.

Nathan was plagued by ongoing troubles. He had difficulty succeeding in business. Once a finicky horse caused his wagon to flip over, destroying his inventory, and he lost his entire investment. He dragged his wife and children around with him under often appalling conditions. Rebecca with a suckling baby and several toddlers went from one place to another with whatever few possessions they took along. Since they changed locations so often in Lowell, they carried with them the little they owned—a few blankets, some pots and pans, and worn-out clothing. Sometimes they found a house to stay in for a few weeks or months, but much of the time they lived in the wagon and ate whatever they could scrounge up. As a dependent woman with very young children, Rebecca had no choice but to stay with her husband and endure, but not without expressing great dissatisfaction with their situation.

Adding up the straight-line distances between the cities and towns, Nathan covered at least a thousand miles (with or without the family), not including any regular trips between towns, retracing steps, peddling into the countryside, or intermittent forays to check out new opportunities. His son, Lou, who remembered these times called him the epitome of the "wandering Jew."

Rebecca's family members disparaged Nathan's tendencies to drift. They derided him, saying that he would never succeed and he was subjecting the family to hardship and suffering. Family members, particularly Rebecca's younger sister Esther Levi and her husband, Max, would send money to get the family out of a bad situation, even though Max had little patience and sympathy for Nathan's rootlessness. They did it for the wellbeing of Rebecca and the children, and not for Nathan's success. A hint of Nathan's intent to find some constancy happened on October 7, 1903, when he became a US citizen. In this case, he used the name "Harry N." on his naturalization card. As Nathan's wife, Rebecca automatically became a citizen.

Shortly after Joey died, Mr. Cohen, Nathan's boss, a tea supplier in Lowell, offered an opportunity to set up a business in Portland, Maine. With life unsettled and insecure, and dealing with the sadness of their child's death, Nathan moved the family to Portland, traveling by horse and wagon. Their third daughter, Lena, was born there on October 14, 1908. The couple opened a little store, which Rebecca ran while Nathan roamed the countryside hawking tea, coffee, and cornstarch. But business never took off, and there were battles between Rebecca and Nathan about the lack of money. Ultimately, the business failed, the horse and wagon were sold to pay the bills, and they came back to Lowell on the train.

Even with this failure, Mr. Cohen still saw something credible in Nathan that prompted him to offer another prospect, this time in Bangor, Maine. Without the horse and wagon, they took the train and moved into a large house on Lincoln Street, near the fair grounds. The family is listed there in the 1910 US Census where Nathan gave his name as William. For a while things were calm for the Goldbergs. They had an inside toilet—a luxury—there was money coming in, and Bessie and Lou entered school, where they made some friends, including a few who were Jewish.

During this time, Nathan became interested in chickens. By raising chickens, he reasoned, he could produce eggs and meat. It was a no-lose proposition. Always hopeful and industrious, he learned how to caponize chickens and set up a neutering business to produce big, fat, tasty birds. When he tried to turn his caponizing technique into a sideshow at the county fair, the authorities closed him down because he didn't have a license. Once again, his new enterprise faded and he and Rebecca started fighting again over money.

Just as they were facing destitution, in 1911, Nathan was offered yet another a chance, this time to rent a chicken farm in Bucksport,

Maine, and he took it. He planned to establish an egg-production business with deliveries by boat to Boston. The family traveled with the usual horse and wagon along with their pots and pans and furniture to a house that looked idyllic. But more disappointment. The house was decrepit. Wind whistled through cracks in the walls and around the windows, and the floors were uneven, making it hard to keep the place clean. There was no indoor plumbing and water had to be carried from a nearby stream. Nathan purchased wood from a vendor and they all transported, split, stacked, and carried it inside for heating and cooking. Again, the older children went to school, and Nathan and Rebecca continued to fight. Once Nathan picked up a chair and beat Rebecca with it. She may have been pregnant at the time. When Lou, who was only eight, tried to protect her, he beat him too.

Around the time that Nathan's egg delivery project began to wane, Rebecca gave birth to her second Joseph on December 5, 1911. Nathan's occupation on the birth certificate was listed as "poultryman." Realizing that his most recent endeavor was failing, he was able to get out of the contract and he and Rebecca made plans to go back to the Boston area. With more than ten years of disappointment, Rebecca had had enough. Imposing her own wishes and fighting for herself and the children's wellbeing, she refused to go back to Lowell. She wanted to be near her family. Nathan yielded and they began the next phase. Nathan and Lou went first to find a place to live in the Boston area. The rest of the family followed soon after and they moved into a walk-up apartment in East Cambridge. With spring approaching, Nathan announced another venture.

Chapter V

WILMINGTON

Contrary to what Rebecca had become accustomed to and contrary to her pessimistic expectations, Nathan's next project ended up having some permanence and potential for the future. After years of crushing hardship and impulsive roving, Nathan had met a land speculator who was selling wooded lots in Wilmington, Massachusetts, about fifteen miles north of Boston. Skeptical, Rebecca protested and argued there was no way to find the money for such a harebrained scheme. After all of Nathan's failed attempts at making a living, she saw this new idea as just another foolish, dead-end proposition. As was customary for the time, she had no influence in his decision; he had already made the deal without asking her. She had to accept it.

For nine dollars down and fifty cents a week he had agreed on a handshake to buy a two-acre piece of property on a still-unnamed Fairview Avenue. He borrowed the money from his boss, Mr. Cohen. It appears that Nathan finally realized that it was time for a permanent home. His vision was to build a house in the country where the air was clean, the family could settle down, they could grow some of their food, and the kids could go to the same school from one year to the next and would have open space to run and explore. Rebecca listened to the plans with disdain. She was trapped: the wife of a wandering dreamer with now five children all age ten and under.

Wilmington in 1910 had a population of 1,858. Even with its growth during the next decade, under any definition, it was a small town. One of its few claims to notoriety was the chance birth of the Baldwin apple in 1740. But, by the early twentieth century, Wilmington already had well established railroad connections south to Boston and Woburn. Woburn was a manufacturing area with leather production as one of its primary industries. Between the mid-1800s and the mid-1900s there were about one hundred tanneries in the area where men and boys worked in physically difficult, dirty, and dangerous conditions caused by the hazardous chemicals used in the tanning process.

Only a few Jews lived in Wilmington and many who already lived there didn't like them. When the Goldbergs moved in, several neighbors moved away because they didn't want to live next door to "Christ killers." From the beginning, the family, especially the children, was subjected to frequent verbal and physical anti-Semitic attacks.

While the family was still living temporarily in East Cambridge, Nathan traveled back and forth to Wilmington with his wagon or on the Boston and Maine Rail Line, bringing construction tools and materials to his new homestead. In the spring of 1912, Nathan and Lou cut down trees and created a clearing to put the house. Nathan arranged for timbers from an old building to be delivered to the site. Within a few months, he with the older children had built a dwelling of wood covered with heavy, black tar paper. They set out a garden plot for peas, corn, potatoes, and tomatoes, and built a two-seat outhouse. They planted apple trees and drove a pipe into the ground until it reached fresh water. In July the whole family moved in. They made arrangements for ice and milk delivery, and Nathan and Lou brought food from Boston. They were even able to harvest their first crop that summer. Over the next months and subsequent years, they built a horse stable and a gigantic chicken coop with an incubator. Nathan made a deal to sell eggs to a wholesaler in Boston.

Slowly, Rebecca softened her stance on the Wilmington scheme. Finally, after ten years of roaming, she began to see the Wilmington venture as a chance to have a secure place to raise the family. In her usual way, she took on the work to make the vision a reality. From early morning to late in the day she physically labored while caring for the children. Even with all of the harsh toil, though, it was far better than being a migrant family living out of a horse-drawn wagon or in temporary housing. Wilmington and neighboring Woburn could offer local job opportunities for the children as they grew. Being established there improved the likelihood of high school graduation. Rebecca highly valued education for both her sons and daughters because of her own lack of schooling. She drilled into her children that not only would they graduate, each would shine as excellent students and be at the top of their class academically. All of the teachers in every grade knew that the Goldberg children were in school to do well. Teachers expected the highest performance from them and they did not disappoint.

Rebecca's strong, long-established Boston connections became a vital, grounding factor in her family's survival. As soon as the chickens began laying eggs, Nathan put his energies into wholesaling while Rebecca and the older kids began delivering farm-fresh eggs to her contacts in and around Boston. They carefully packed eggs in suitcases, took the train into Boston, and walked or rode trains or above-ground trolleys to make distributions to Chelsea and Boston neighborhoods—the North End, West End, South End, Dorchester, and Roxbury. Visiting her customers once or twice a week allowed Rebecca to earn some money, barter crops for essential goods, and keep up to date on what was going on in the Wernick clan.

The entire Goldberg family worked to make the homestead succeed. The older kids, Bessie, Lou, and Minnie, helped build structures, worked the garden, and tended the chickens. Nathan toiled feverishly clearing land and finishing the house. Being unafraid of very hard work, Rebecca pumped and carried endless buckets of water to make cement for chicken coop walls. She collected vegetables to cook or sell and made lots of scrambled eggs and chicken for dinner. In between all of her work, she was still able to develop cautious friendships with neighbors, some of whom were also immigrants from Eastern Europe, although not Jewish. She conversed in Polish, which she had spoken in the old country and gradually developed a local cadre of both English and non-English speaking acquaintances. Nathan kept a part-time job in East Cambridge and continued to schmooze with people to ferret out a new deal.

Between 1911 and 1915, Rebecca avoided

having another—her last—child. Edward, the youngest of the Goldberg children, was born in Wilmington on January 23, 1915. In the early years of her marriage, she had had four children in rapid succession. There was a gap of almost three years between the next two children, and another four years before Eddie was born. Rebecca must have figured out a way to reduce the number of pregnancies or births. There was virtually no birth control available to American women, especially poor women, because the 1873 Comstock Act prohibited distributing information and materials related to contraception. Rebecca had already borne all of her children by the time Margaret Sanger opened her first family planning and birth control clinic in New York in 1916. For this, Sanger was brought to trial and spent thirty days in a work house for distributing family planning literature. There was little if any similar accessible information in Boston.

Rebecca may have gotten birth control advice from family members, but seeing an expensive doctor was out of reach. Medical services, even if available, would have been unaffordable, and, even then, the advice given may have been faulty. Women talked to each other about simple techniques, but these were usually unreliable or unsafe. Breastfeeding offered natural birth control as women tend not to ovulate while nursing a baby. Perhaps Rebecca used the rhythm method suggested by the Catholic Church. Rebecca's close relatives may have had access to this information and passed it on. But, even if the method was understood, it required that a woman knew how to calculate her fertile times and her husband had to be willing to abstain from sexual intercourse for about a week each month. Costly condoms and coitus interruptus were all possible, but the man had to agree to use them. Sponges or vaginal caps were obtainable, but expensive. Vaginal douches and squatting after intercourse were also common, but undependable. Then there was abortion, but laws about abortion were extremely restrictive. Still, a woman could have an abortion by medical professionals if they had money, by back-alley laypeople, or they could try to give themselves an abortion.

Different methods women used to try to induce an abortion included strong, medically prescribed drugs; potent herbs; vigorous exercise; very hot steam baths; douches; objects placed in the vagina; and pens, quills, or needles inserted into the uterus through the cervix or even through the abdominal wall, all of which were ineffective or very dangerous. Without access to medical care and with at least one unwanted pregnancy, Rebecca gave herself an abortion using a hatpin, most likely a long, wooden one. Many women died as a result of illicit or self-inflicted abortions. Rebecca was lucky.

With this as the backdrop of what their lives were like, over time, the family's income and situation began to improve a bit. With the extra financial security from Nathan's work in Boston and jobs that he did in local tanneries, the tar paper house was finished, and the crops and chicken population were productive.

Everything was looking up, and for three years there was a period of relative calm, until calamity struck. One morning in the fall of 1915, Nathan woke early to go to work. When he lit the stove to heat the house, some nearby material burst into flame and quickly burned out of control. Nathan and Rebecca, with baby

Eddie in her arms, managed to get all of the other children out safely. But there was no way to stop the fire—within minutes the wood and tar paper house was ablaze. Someone ran to the fire chief's house, but by the time the firefighters arrived with a horse hitched to the fire wagon, the house and everything in it was totally consumed.

Everything was lost, except for the sturdy iron stove, some pots and pans, and some laundry drying on the lines in the yard. A family picture was taken by an unknown photographer right after the fire. Mostly everyone is smiling but, without understanding the story, an observer would not know the destruction that had happened there. With nowhere to go, they moved into the chicken coop.

FAMILY, outside with stove
Family Photo

Once again, the Goldbergs started over, but fortunately they didn't have to move because they owned the land and could stay on it, even if they had to live in a chicken coop. Nathan's decision to buy land and build a house proved to be exceedingly fortunate. Undaunted, Nathan kept moving on with his plans. He obtained a loan of seven hundred dollars from the Woburn Cooperative Bank and set to work on a new, grander, two-story house, with many bedrooms. Nathan rose at 4:30 each morning, roused Lou, who was now eleven years old, and together they worked on the house until it was time for school. Lou resumed his labors after the school day. There was a never-ending number of things to get done. At times, Nathan's anger erupted if Lou didn't complete his chores and would hit him, once with a wooden two-by-four, leaving him in pain for days.

NATHAN, in overalls
Family Photo

The general economy was improving, particularly when the US entered World War I in April 1917. Jobs had become available for Nathan in war plants in neighboring towns so there was additional income. Finally, after so many years the house was close to completion by 1918. What a great accomplishment. It had a big porch, a kitchen, living and dining rooms, four or five bedrooms upstairs, and an indoor bathroom, which was still a luxury then. Rebecca's demanding workdays didn't change as the garden, chicken and egg production, and children's education continued. Still, she was cautious about assuming everything would be financially secure.

After a number of years of living in Wilmington, Rebecca had adjusted to country life and being entrepreneurial in her own right, she began to see another opportunity. People from Boston were starting to come to Wilmington's Silver Lake for a day's or weekend's outing. Silver Lake with its swimming beaches, park areas, summer-time food, dancing, and boating was becoming a destination. It was easily reachable because of already established train lines.

Rebecca began to realize that her almost completed house with its many bedrooms could be a destination for her family and friends. Her children could easily vacate their beds for short periods and she could rent out their bedrooms. Just like Silver Lake, the Goldberg house was an easy trip from North Station by train. She would offer a getaway place in the country, but now for Jews. She got the word out through her regular Boston egg route customers and, in the warmer months, relatives and friends began to visit what became known as the *Palace in the Woods.* The Wernick sisters came with their husbands and children along with friends like the Helperns. Others like the Schlossberg family also came. They owned a bakery on Barton Street in the West End. Just as the Helperns had helped with jobs in difficult times, the Schlossbergs had sent out to Wilmington rag bags filled with bread that the children picked up at the local train station.

Rebecca charged for the rooms, quantities of Jewish-style food, and the clean country air. Along with freshly prepared meals, she served up her homemade blueberry wine produced from the wild high- and low-bush varieties that the children picked in the vast patches near the house. To make her wine, Rebecca boiled the berries with sugar and water and added ethyl alcohol. Obtaining the alcohol was no problem and there were no restrictions as Prohibition was still a few years away. Everyone who vacationed there loved her blueberry wine, especially the men. On these weekend escapes, the women roamed the nearby woods and fields during the day, sharing confidences, and overseeing the children. The men congregated, staying up all night playing poker, smoking cigarettes or cigars, and drinking plenty of Rebecca's wine.

In her characteristic way, Rebecca worked tirelessly, now catering to paying guests, putting in long hours which were interspersed with a few moments of camaraderie. She found time to sit and talk with familiar friends and relatives speaking both in Yiddish and English and using the two languages to make jokes and puns. She even appeared to be enjoying herself, although she would have had trouble acknowledging that. Her experience had taught her that something bad could happen at any moment. Shuffling these darker thoughts aside, she loved being in charge of orchestrating the activities in what became a successful enterprise.

The Palace in the Woods was thriving and life was much better. Yet, soon, there was another major catastrophe. In 1918, with the roof on the new house not completely finished, Nathan died.

Chapter VI

WIDOWHOOD

On the evening of September 16, 1918, Nathan set out for his job at a war manufacturing plant in North Woburn. It was Yom Kippur, the holiest day of the Jewish year. Lou described what happened that day.

It was twilight. Most of us were in the kitchen, our favorite room, watching the sunset. A car stopped in front of the house. A dark figure of a man stepped out of the car, stood for a moment as if surveying the area, and then came towards the porch. Of course, we were curious. Maybe the person was lost. He picked up speed as he approached the front door. By that time, Ma and I were waiting for him at the entrance. He spoke slowly and deliberately. "Mrs. Goldberg, I have bad news for you. Your husband has been in a railroad accident. He is at Massachusetts General Hospital in the West End. Come, I will drive you there."

In the South Wilmington railyard, Nathan had been run over by a switcher engine. The accident severed both of his legs. A switcher is a small locomotive used for assembling and disassembling trains, and for moving railroad cars from one place to another. The engine that struck Nathan was going quite slowly, wending its way around the train yard maze. The train operator did not have the time to stop when Nathan appeared on the tracks in front of the engine. Knowing that Nathan had been run over, he was able to get word quickly to J.P. Bixby, M.D., who was the doctor that served the New England Manufacturing Company, Nathan's employer. Nathan was placed on a train to Boston and was still alive when he arrived at the hospital. The front-page headlines in the *Boston Daily Globe* of September 17, 1918, Morning Edition were about WWI peace attempts and the Spanish Flu. On the bottom of page 14, the last page of this edition, there was a report of the accident:

RUSSIAN'S LEGS SEVERED

WOBURN. Sept. 16—Nathan Goldberg, a Russian, 45 years old, of Fairview Ave, Wilmington, who works on the night shift at the New England Manufacturing Company, North Woburn, was run over by a switching engine at the South Wilmington station at 5 o'clock today. Both legs were severed below the knees.

Goldberg had just stepped from a B&M train and was on way to his work. Dr. J. P. Bixby rendered first aid and the wounded man was sent by train to the Massachusetts General Hospital.

From the *Boston Daily Globe*, September 17, 1918, Morning Edition, Page 14

Rebecca and Lou, who was now fourteen, went with the man in his car. Bessie, the oldest daughter, stayed to take care of the other children. Nathan was heavily bandaged but awake when they got to the hospital. "*Vos machst du* [How are you], Nissan?" Rebecca asked gently. "*Nisht gut* [not good]," he replied with great difficulty. He was able to tell Lou how terrible the pain was. The transfusions, one of which came from his son, couldn't replace all of the blood he had lost, and he died at 10:00 p.m., about five hours after the accident. His wife and son were both in the room when staff pulled the white sheet over his face.

In shock, Rebecca and Lou left the hospital, walked to nearby North Station, and took the 11:00 p.m. train back to Wilmington to tell the family. Rebecca found a way to get word of Nathan's death to the Wernicks, and Simon made arrangements to bring Nathan's body to the South End to prepare it for interment.

The next day, after an agonizing and sleepless night, Rebecca, Lou, and Bessie walked back to the South Wilmington station in the pre-dawn darkness. Thirteen-year-old Minnie stayed home with Lena, Joseph, and Eddie. They took the 6:00 a.m. train back to North Station and walked the few miles to the Wernick apartment on Compton Street. They talked very little. The idea that their husband and father was dead was inconceivable. Suddenly, Nathan, a powerhouse of a man, full of energy and bluster, was gone. He was forty-five years old.

At Simon's apartment, Nathan's body was prepared for the funeral by the *chevra kadisha*. As Lou watched, members of this Jewish burial society washed his mangled body in the prescribed manner, holding him up, turning him one way and then another, reciting biblical passages and blessings at each stage in the ritual cleansing process. As required by tradition, they gathered all of the bloody clothing and bandages and placed them in a plain pine coffin along with Nathan's bodily remains.

Insensitive to the family's grief, Simon's intolerance spilled out. He ranted with loathing that Nathan had gone to work on Yom Kippur, and his extreme attitudes continued being displayed throughout the day. In the cortège to the cemetery in Woburn, Simon insisted that Lou travel in the hearse and not in the car with the rest of the family. Lou, unnerved, fixated on the contents of the casket, wondering if his father's legs were in there also. The image of his father's body and the basket of blood-stained garments haunted him for the rest of his life. At the funeral, Simon made it clear that he didn't consider his grandson to be a real Jew because of his lack of Jewish education and a bar mitzvah, which his grandfather believed he should have had the year before at age thirteen. He called him a "Christ" and would not allow Lou's coat lapel to be torn in the traditional, sacred sign of mourning.

The rest of the Goldberg family returned to Wilmington, and in the days after the funeral, a sense of devastation and despair swept over them all. How would they manage without a husband and father? Of course, Eddie was only two-and-a-half years old and had no memories of this tragic moment.

With Nathan's death, Rebecca instantly lost a large portion of the family's income, as well as the security of having a man at home. As mercurial as his personality had been and even in light of the trials to which he subjected Rebecca and his children, Nathan had toiled assiduously to support and protect the family. He stayed with them, never abandoning his responsibility.

Almost immediately, and with her survival instinct and tenacity intact, Rebecca knew that even with this overpowering tragedy there was no time to sit idle with worry. Her job now was to assume leadership, take over decision-making, and continue doing what needed to be done. The roof had to be completed. Chickens needed tending, eggs had to be gathered and brought to Boston. The younger children, Eddie; Joseph, age six; and Lena, age ten, required their mother's care. The mortgage payment was due every month. Winter was coming and they needed fuel to heat the house, for cooking, and to warm the water for washing dishes and bathing. There were the household chores of preparing meals, cleaning, sweeping, and laundry. Rebecca knew instinctively that these basic responsibilities were to keep them all focused and set out a practical, daily path to follow. By doing this and maintaining their routines, one step after another, they would endure this overwhelming loss.

There were some things that Rebecca had no control over. Outside forces intruded their privacy. Prosthetics manufacturers must have seen the report of Nathan's accident in the newspaper and they bombarded the household with advertisements for false legs and crutches, presenting a cynical suggestion that their father would walk again and be a contributing family member. The older children tried to intercept the ads and shield Rebecca from reminders that Nathan was dead.

Local citizens collected staples and coal for the family. Rebecca rejected all of the food because it included leftover pork and beans from a community supper. "They're giving us pork and beans!?" she protested, but she kept the coal. The Town of Wilmington offered Rebecca financial assistance. She refused. She had been told that if she accepted charity from the Town of Wilmington that the older children, Bessie and Lou, would have had to leave school and get jobs. She would have none of it. "Never!" she said. "They are going to graduate from high school."

Nathan's employer the New England Manufacturing Company, collected about eight hundred dollars from employees, and she accepted it. Family and friends offered help and she accepted that as well. The Boston and Maine Railroad initially offered $500 in compensation, but by 1920, with the help of a lawyer, there was a settlement of $1,400. The family never thought that was enough and the railroad never admitted responsibility. It claimed that Nathan had mistakenly gotten off on the wrong side of the train and walked between two stationary cars into the path of the switcher engine.

Now a widow with six children, Rebecca assessed her situation. She had the small income from her egg business, her summertime earnings from guests, and intermittent assistance from her extended family. The summer was over and she would have to wait until next spring to continue her Palace in the Woods. She knew this would never be enough. Even with her staunch determination, at times she felt so desperate that she considered taking all of her children to the river, holding their heads under water, and then drowning herself. She didn't or couldn't do that, of course, because her older children would have prevented her. But, oh, the desolation that led her to contemplate such an absolute act.

As autumn continued, she began to think about next steps. In the spring she would plant another garden and sell corn, peas, potatoes, and lettuce. Next summer she would again provide a country getaway for city friends. Despite the devastating loss, it became remarkably clear that Rebecca was undaunted. She had no choice. As much as her parents and siblings cared about her, they were also struggling, and none would have been able to take in a widow with six children. She utterly rejected the possibility that some of her children could be taken away and placed with other families or even in an orphanage. The alternatives of destitution and breaking up the family were unthinkable. Rebecca told Lou that he would now be the father and above all he had to obey her. "Ma knows best," she said. Her few decisive words demonstrated the confidence she had in her ability to take control.

Despite hand-me-down clothes from relatives and money from the older children's small after-school jobs, it was nearly impossible to make ends meet. Rebecca knew that determination was not enough. In addition to daily food and supplies, she had to finish the roof. She needed more money.

Chapter VII

ENTERING THE WORLD OF ILLEGAL ALCOHOL

Because Eddie was the youngest child and not yet in school when his father died, he continued to accompany Rebecca on her egg route. He grew up with memories of his mother dressed modestly for travel, a suitcase full of eggs in one hand, and his own small hand in the other. At the age of three or four he witnessed the tentative beginning of her journey into the mysterious world of illicit alcohol sales. He was there when his mother stashed the first gallon of raw alcohol in her suitcase after completing her egg route.

It all began just a few months after Nathan's death. During a visit to Chelsea, a relative, egg client, and one who understood Rebecca's situation suggested, "Becky, Prohibition is coming. Why don't you start selling alcohol in Wilmington? You would have many customers out there in the woods. Men always want a drink after a hard day's work. You could make a few extra dollars." He revealed that he could supply her with the raw alcohol that he was making in his basement. She could mix in liquids and flavors, put it in bottles, and sell it out of her house. As one of her Palace in the Woods guests, he had sampled her famous blueberry wine. "You already know how to make the wine," he said. "The other drinks are easy; I will teach you."

WHOLE COUNTRY GOES DRY

The American Issue, Westerville, Ohio, January 25, 1919, Page 1

At the beginning of 1919, and as everyone knew and expected, the Dry Act—the Volstead Act— was ratified on January 16. One year later, on January 17, 1920, Prohibition went into effect. This twelve-month period gave people the chance to buy and hide quantities of their alcohol inventories; get rid of existing stashes; figure out how to get around production, transport, and sales bans; or to make their own booze.

The year of grace also gave Rebecca a little while to think about what she should do. She was cautious, being afraid to take any risks that could put herself and her children's welfare in jeopardy. In the worst case she could be deported and the family could fall apart. It took many months and conversations to decide. Not knowing where this new endeavor would lead, she ultimately recognized that it would be a simple way to get more cash and she could tolerate the danger. Luck was likely on her side. She had her own trusted alcohol supplier and also had her small Wilmington network that knew and was sympathetic to her plight. She decided to take a chance.

One day, after completing her sales route, she went back to her friend's Chelsea apartment, packed a gallon jug of homemade spirits in her suitcase, and brought it home on the train. Everything looked as normal as on any other trip. Here was this thin woman in a worn, dark skirt and tightly wrapped shawl with a suitcase, and a young child. No one, including the familiar railroad conductors and other people she knew and greeted would have suspected anything unusual about Mrs. Goldberg. Her normally light return-trip suitcase was heavy, but Rebecca was exceedingly strong from almost a decade of hard labor on the Wilmington farmstead, and she deftly managed the weight.

Walking more quickly and with a bit more purpose than usual, Rebecca made her way home, hustling Eddie along. She was nervous because she knew that Prohibition was not to be taken lightly. She was relieved when she reached her house, knowing her children would find good hiding places. This was the beginning of Rebecca's career as a bootlegger. With so many others, she became a small part of the vast illegal alcohol process. Well before Prohibition was enacted, people had started to determine how to manufacture and trade alcohol in defiance of the law. The challenge was how to avoid getting caught.

The enactment of Prohibition came after more than one hundred years of effort by individuals and groups that condemned hard drink on the moral grounds that it destroyed the fabric of family life. Some religious groups, often Protestant and Evangelical, considered excessive drinking a sin. There were numerous anti-alcohol and anti-saloon advocates, including the Woman's Christian Temperance Union and the Anti-Saloon League, each with its own approach to making America dry. Their concerns had some validity. Poverty and destitution were widespread, and alcohol abuse was one of the contributing factors. Women were especially impacted by the prevalence of excessive drinking. Men would spend their earnings on drink and not on food and security for the family. It was too common that some men regularly used alcohol to excess, ultimately abandoning wives and children. Frequently, addiction prevailed over family needs. This situation had never been one of Rebecca's problems. Nathan did not drink alcohol to any extent. He had simply and tragically died by accident, leaving Rebecca a widow.

Those opposed to Prohibition were the "wets." They argued that the legislation infringed on individual and religious rights. Beer and whiskey manufacturers, distributors, and saloon owners and their patrons contested prohibition. Businessmen with a stake in the industry argued that their incomes and their right to conduct business would be unjustly curtailed by the ban. The chance to make a lot of money at every step in the process created profit-making arenas to be guarded and defended at all costs.

Everyone in the entire alcohol chain would feel the law's impact, and the sequence was long and intricate. Within this web was the production of raw ingredients (wheat, rye, barley, malt, fruit, and yeast); the various systems to move raw materials all over the country; big and small alcohol manufacturers; producers of the equipment needed in the steps of the process; bottling and storage facilities; distribution through vast transportation channels; and end-of-the-line sales. Everyone at every stage of this process faced a very uncertain future and potential financial loss was prodigious.

The acceptance or rejection of the Volstead act generally split along religious or cultural lines. Catholics used wine for communion and Jews as part of the Sabbath, Passover, and other holy rituals. Catholics and Jews tended to be against Prohibition. They argued that religious rights, a foundational American entitlement, were being denied. Alcohol production was somewhat divided by ethnicity. Beer was largely controlled by German manufacturers and sellers. Whiskey distilling was often in the purview of Jews.

Although the law incorporated a broad swath, it did provide exceptions to the ban. Religious ritual, preserving fruit, and a doctor's prescription were the main exemptions, and Prohibition opponents used these exceptions broadly to defend their use of alcoholic drinks.

Making pure alcohol was one of the easiest ways to get into illegal production. Raw alcohol could be diluted by mixing it with other liquids. Stills that produced whiskey, rye, or gin were more complicated, needing ingredients such as barley, wheat, rye, corn, or potatoes, and more complicated equipment.

Ironically, although the law prohibited most production, the means for making pure alcohol were readily available. All one needed was water, sugar, and yeast—preferably brewer's yeast—but baker's yeast would do. With some different size clean containers, tubing, netting to cover the equipment, and a place to hide the apparatus until it foamed and formed into one hundred percent ethanol, anyone could make illicit liquor, and small operations were easy to hide.

Things could go wrong in a now-unregulated environment. Home-brewed alcohol might contain significant impurities that could blind or kill, for example. But, not surprisingly, the impetus to make liquor was robust and production flourished under veils of secrecy, covert conversations, whispered passwords, and backdoor deals.

People became extraordinarily creative. They built stills in the middle of forests and in abandoned warehouses. They created gin in bathtubs and, like Rebecca's contact in Chelsea, clandestinely made ethanol in any space where they could hide the equipment. Big ships anchored outside of the two-mile international boundaries where they off-loaded barrels and bottles onto smaller boats that carried this cargo to beaches and coves along the thousands of miles of United States shoreline. Complicated systems were put in place to bring alcohol across the Canadian and Mexican borders. Crime syndicates had control over broad bands of production, distributions, and sales. Speakeasies abounded and were easy to find and enter. Alcoholic drinks made their way into private homes and clandestine saloons. Lots of people made a lot of money, had a good time, and sometimes got killed if they stepped into someone else's territory.

Despite its legal status, Prohibition suffered from a lack of effective and adequate enforcement. There were few, if any, formal systems to flush out small operations like Rebecca's. Opponents of drinking had underestimated the difficulty of trying to legislate morality in an American culture that valued freedom of thought, independence, and individual rights. They also did not anticipate the creativity and entrepreneurial spirit which drove people to find ways around the law. It was Rebecca's small, local setup that gave her an advantage and made her a tiny, almost invisible speck within an enormous rebellious and innovative movement that was dedicated to maintaining America as a drinking nation.

Although Rebecca may not have known the history, alcohol had been a part of US society since the revolution. George Washington loved Madeira. He acknowledged the benefit of liquor for his troops and, starting in 1782, soldiers were given a daily ration of whiskey. James Madison drank a pint of whiskey a day. Thomas Jefferson had a vast wine cellar and made his own rye whiskey. Legendary Johnny Appleseed roamed Ohio and Indiana, distributing apple seeds to boost production of hard cider in the late eighteenth to the mid-nineteenth century.

When we think of Prohibition now, it conjures up familiar images of federal agents smashing barrels full of whiskey and rye, heavily guarded speakeasy doorways with small windows for a sentinel to ask who wanted to enter, stills hidden away in dark, tangled woods, and flappers in their 1920s dresses secreting small flasks in their lacy garters. Period films depict gangsters flouting the law, wheeling and dealing, and killing each other over money and control. Small numbers of people made millions of dollars in the shadow of the law in a universe of corruption and deceit.

These widespread, often romantic impressions of this era did not reflect Rebecca's world. She was not a flapper, did not run a speakeasy, did not dance the Charleston in a fringed sheath. She did not have a secreted still, nor did she belong to a crime syndicate or make a lot of money. She was a little Jewish woman in clean, but very worn clothing who chose to defy the law and overcome fears of prison or deportation, only driven by a mother's imperative to feed her children.

With that first gallon, she expanded her free enterprise endeavors from eggs to booze and became part of the underbelly of the alcohol trade. Her operation was quite simple: a little raw ethanol with a high proportion of liquid to thin it and a few clandestine customers. In the realm of bottles and barrels, she was at the very bottom.

Rebecca's operation was a true family affair. The children, no matter how young, participated in the procurement of raw ingredients and beverage production. She had no compunction in involving them; they were all in it together. When she was not in school, Lena helped carry home gallon bottles of alcohol from Chelsea. All of the children collected wild high-bush and low-bush blueberries from patches that stretched for acres near their house. Because each variety ripened at different times, there was a consistent supply during the spring and summer. Eddie searched for empty bottles on the side of the road or in the dump, rejoicing when he could bring a few home to his mother, especially if they were small enough to fit into a man's pocket. Lou devised a spot under a tar paper flap in the chicken coop to hide bottles once they had been filled. The children were proud of their clever deceptions. The younger ones may not have fully under-stood that they were complicit in breaking the law and the older kids did what their mother told them to do.

From her earlier days as the proprietor of the Palace in the Woods, Rebecca knew well how to craft her traditional blueberry wine until it was the right consistency, color, and taste. She knew what people liked. The main difference was that she was now purchasing alcohol ille-gally rather than previously from a perfectly legitimate source, perhaps the local pharmacist. For her other drinks, she mixed the raw spirits with water, dipping a finger into each batch until it tasted just right. She didn't have a measured recipe, just her own instincts and a little guidance from her Chelsea source. She needed very few ingredients. With just water, the product was clear and looked like gin. If she added a little browned sugar, it looked like whiskey. Customers didn't seem to worry about the flavor, only the effect.

Rebecca's first customer was a Wilmington painter whom she already knew. In a conversation one day Rebecca cautiously let him know that she had some drinks for sale and he bought a pint. He came back a few days later for more and, in the meantime, had told a few of his friends that she was selling. Unlike her Boston egg customers, these buyers were strictly local. In this small town, word got around quickly. Her customer base gradually grew, but she was perpetually wary and vigilant, only selling to people she knew or their friends, always asking, "What do you want? Who sent you?" They came to her back door, usually at the end of the work day, and she sold them pints for $1.00 or $1.25 each—a lot of money in those days. The Goldberg Palace in the Woods became known around town as the *Tavern in the Woods*, and business blossomed. She began to enjoy the bantering, conspiratorial conversations, and edgy relationships in this clandestine environment. Her clientele represented a broad base of people in the community, from working men to civic leaders. Mostly customers came to the house, but some prominent community citizens wanted their goods delivered so as not to risk being seen. Again, the children helped out. Lena would tuck a quart of "whiskey" into her big overcoat and bring it to the chief of police.

The names of other customers have been lost, but the passed-down stories suggest that there were many. For about four years, life for the Goldbergs was good, and breaking the law became routine, but tempered with a lot of caution. They had struggled for every penny in the past and now had more cash coming in than ever before. It was wonderful. Finally, there was a little more money to help raise their standard of living. They were able to purchase new clothes instead of relying on hand-me-downs. They could buy their own bread rather than depend on bakery contributions from the West End. The children could go to the movies once in a while. Rebecca was proud of her self-sufficiency and her improved financial situation. She also had some income from the older children who were now working in various jobs after school and during the summer. For about four or five years, anyone naively looking in on the Goldberg home would have seen a calm, organized existence: a hardworking widow; chicken, egg, and garden produce production and sales; children in school; and summertime guests to whom she probably still served blueberry wine. They would not have seen the daily alcohol production and late afternoon and evening criminal transactions. It is not known whether Rebecca's family in Boston knew about her sideline, but there is no indication that they tried to stop her.

It wasn't until the mid-1920s that the federal government began pressuring local communities to enforce the Volstead Act. Wilmington's police force had insufficient personnel to find dealers scattered in the surrounding woods. To increase their capability to administer the law, the town selectmen hired "spotters"—temporary agents—who were paid to entrap bootleggers.

One evening in early August of 1925, two of these hired detectives came to Rebecca's back door and attempted to buy a bottle. Ever suspicious, she chatted with them in her guarded style as she tried to figure out who they were and who had sent them. She refused a direct sale, but left a half-pint on the step for them to take after she closed the door, with the agreement that they would leave money. The next morning, the bottle was gone and 75 cents was on the stoop.

Within days of that encounter there was a raid on the Goldberg home when Wilmington police arrived and combed the house. They found a few bottles of blueberry wine and some beer (that she must have gotten from another source), but they missed bigger stashes that were hidden in the base of the dining table and in the chicken coop.

Rebecca was not the only bootlegger in Wilmington when she, along with other alleged area rum-runners, was summoned to appear in court before a judge on August 11, 1925. Word of her summons reached her family in Boston and, again stepping in to help, they hired a good defense lawyer, Harry Levowich. In preparation for the hearing, he coached Rebecca to say that she had some wine on a doctor's prescription for her sick daughter, a perfectly legal defense. Mr.

Levowich gently guided her to the front of the courtroom to stand before judge Jesse Morton. The lawyer told the judge that she pleaded "not guilty" and in a brilliant strategic move, he engaged Chief of Police Hill as a character witness. Front-page articles in the *Boston Daily Globe* and the *Woburn Daily Times* provide an account of what happened that day.

THE BOSTON DAILY GLOBE
AUGUST 11, 1925

"JUDGE TURNS DOWN SPOTTER EVIDENCE: Morton frees Wilmington Rum Case Defendants, Saying Detectives Hired by Selectmen Lied.

The first case was that of Rebecca Goldberg, alleging the sale of liquor to [Detective] Forest. She denied that she had ever seen either of the detectives in her life. Judge Morton questioned Forest sharply as to why he went to the Goldberg house at 11 o'clock at night when he knew there were no men in the house. Forest answered that he was making the rounds of the suspected cases and came to Goldberg's last. Judge Morton declared it seemed strange to him and Mrs. Goldberg was found "not guilty."

From *The Boston Daily Globe*, August 11, 1925, Page 1

THE WOBURN DAILY TIMES

AUGUST 11, 1925

"First Wilmington Liquor Case Dismissed by Court

Judge Jesse W. Morton Frowns upon "Spotter" Evidence. Chief Called by Defense

The case was one of the most unusual cases in the history of the local [Woburn, MA] court. The fact that the defense council, Harry P. Levowich of Boston, called Chief of Police Walter A. Hill to the stand as a character witness for the accused, was the unusual feature of the case. Chief Hill said that he had known Mrs. Goldberg for ten years and her reputation in the community was good. When asked if he had known of her ever indulging in the sale of liquor, the chief said that he had heard people say so, but he had never secured any evidence from an authentic source."

From *The Woburn Daily Times*, August 11, 1925, Page 1

Of course, the defendant, her lawyer, and the police chief were lying. Rebecca had been producing and selling alcoholic beverages for a number of years, her lawyer knew she was dealing in booze, and the chief of police was a client. The hired detectives actually admitted deceit in securing the evidence, and they were discredited because of their unseemly tactic of visiting the home of a respected widow late in the evening. Other alcohol suits were heard that day and all were dismissed. In the Wilmington Police Department History of Important Dates, 1925 is cited as a big year for the seizure of illegal alcohol. Although not specifically mentioned in that record, Rebecca was among the perpetrators.

Family ties, established local relationships, community sympathy, and crafty tactics were on Rebecca's side. As was their habit, her family came to her rescue in this most trying situation. People in the community respected and had sympathy for her even though she was a criminal in the eyes of the law. She had gotten in and then out of illegal actions at the right time. When Prohibition was enacted, there were grossly inadequate provisions for enforcement. Lawlessness abounded throughout the country because there were nowhere near enough officers to cover the limitless small operations in houses and wooded areas, or on drop-off locations on thousands of coastal beaches, or on complex trade routes, or the huge, powerful criminal systems. Rebecca benefited greatly from inadequate national law enforcement resources and the corruption of local authorities.

Many years later, Rebecca's children would smile and chuckle about their mother's foray into dealing in booze. They told the stories over and over again. Along with this amusement, however, there was an undercurrent of sorrow about what their mother and they had gone through just to keep them all together and survive. They were proud of being creative participants in an illicit adventure, but any romantic or humorous overlay that the story took on was possible only because they had escaped serious consequences.

Rebecca never had to face her parents and explain her court summons. Simon had died on January 17, 1923. Anna died on January 6, 1925, about six months before Rebecca's court date.

Chapter VIII

LIFE AFTER PROHIBITION

After the court hearing, Rebecca and her children returned to the house on Fairview Avenue. As was their habit, they didn't talk much about what had happened. They went back to their regular routines of work and school, and Rebecca knew she had to make a decision. Should she continue to sell alcohol and live with the risk, or should she stop? Even though Rebecca was a citizen, intolerant attitudes abounded against immigrants during the 1920s. The anti-alcohol movement blamed the abuse of alcohol on émigrés from Southern and Eastern Europe, which included Jews. Although deportation was unlikely for a lone fifty-year-old widow, the threat was present and she, as a foreigner from Eastern Europe, was aware and worried.

Although she had influential friends in town, Rebecca realized that things had changed. She sensed that the battle against illegal alcohol was about to begin in earnest, and she didn't want to take any chances, even though it would be two more years before there was serious federal attempt to enforce the Volstead Act. In 1927, Eliot Ness joined the US Treasury Department and began working with the Bureau of Prohibition to identify, prosecute, and imprison offenders. Ness was focused on big criminals like Al Capone and crime syndicates, and not on widow Rebecca Goldberg in the Wilmington woods. Still, the potential for punishment was there. She decided to stop her operation and went back to selling eggs and hosting city visitors who would still come to the country for warm days and overnights. Blueberry wine was no longer served. With her retirement from the trade, her fear of capture was over, but she missed the gentle intrigue and the companionship of her old customers, her criminal co-conspirators. Prohibited

BACK ROW: Bessie, Rebecca, Minnie
KNEELING IN FRONT: Lou, Eddie, Joe
(*Note: Lena is not present in this photograph*)
Family Photo

alcohol had gotten Rebecca through some of the most difficult periods.

The children were becoming adults, and Rebecca could see her vision of having educated children coming to fruition. During and after her illegal alcohol business, the children began to complete high school. Bessie graduated in 1920 and went to work. Lou completed school in 1922, and when he was accepted to college, his tuition was supported by a prominent New York cousin. Even while in school, Lou worked summers and at odd jobs. Minnie graduated in 1924 and began a varied work career that included buying and selling antiques. In 1926, Lena graduated and worked as a secretary in Boston. The older children were out in the world working. They lived at home and commuted on trains to local or Boston-area jobs.

Her two remaining sons, Joe and Eddie, were star students and on their way to obtaining diplomas.

By the time Rebecca was done with illicit trafficking, her life had become secure through the contributions of her children. She accepted, actually expected, the weekly cash additions to the family's finances, but she wanted very little else for herself. When her kids tried to give her a fancy dress, she rejected it, saying that all she wanted was a new housedress.

The times were changing in other ways. The advent and popularity of the automobile gave travelers the opportunity to visit more distant and less accessible locations than they could by train. Wilmington's Silver Lake had fewer and fewer visitors, and Rebecca felt the same shift as her weekend business waned when people began to travel to New Hampshire or Maine for their vacations.

Looking back on Rebecca's life, her stalwart personality dominates. But she had an extremely significant advantage during a time when the possibility of a widow losing a place to live and her children being dispersed was not uncommon. Fortunately, Rebecca's ability to survive was largely because of Nathan's legacy of a house and land. Owning property meant that this land and house were hers. As long as she continued to make loan payments, no one could remove her from her rightful place or take over this precious asset. No one could raise her rent or evict her. It allowed her freedom from worry about ever having to find new places to live. Upon this acreage, she was able to plant herself and her family, and sprout. It gave her solidity and a firm platform from which she could do what was necessary for survival. As difficult as life was, her ownership accorded enough freedom to explore multiple channels for achieving self-reliance.

Chapter IX

THE FINAL YEARS

The remaining years of Rebecca's life were financially stable, mostly peaceful, but punctuated with discord and more tragedy. Her children's passage into adulthood created a mixture of gratification and tension. As the children strove to create their own lives, Rebecca's unremitting efforts to keep control over them ultimately generated disappointment and sadness in her. Each child, in his or her own way, sought to break the power she had exerted over them for so many years. She didn't accept these changes easily.

The first in the series of disillusionments involved Lou, who was accepted into Massachusetts Agricultural College (Mass Aggie), now the University of Massachusetts, Amherst. Lou struggled in college, but managed to graduate after a few academic setbacks. His graduation was affirming for Rebecca. Not only did she have high school graduates, she had one child with a college degree.

For graduation, Lou's sponsor came from New York and rented a taxi to take the family to the university campus in Amherst about one hundred miles away. They had a joyful celebration back home in Wilmington after the ceremony. Rebecca had assumed that Lou would remain in Wilmington and become the designated family support and leader. But he had other ideas. Within a year of his graduation, he left for California, leaving everyone stunned and feeling that he had deserted them all. He had dreamed of independence and having an adventure on the West Coast. His vision faded because he had trouble finding a lasting job and felt discrimination because he was a recognizable Jew with the Goldberg name. He legally changed his name to Gilbert, thinking that would shield him. It didn't, however, and within a year, and because of a lack of cash, he desolately wired the family for money to bring him home. His return was met with suspicion and anger. Everyone grudgingly accepted him back into the family, but the hurt remained. Rebecca never forgave him for abandoning her and his siblings and for spoiling her dream. When Lou married, Rebecca was cool and kept her distance from him along with his wife, Anne, and their two small children, her only grandchildren. Perhaps as a way to make amends, throughout his life, Lou frequently expressed deep respect for his mother's strength.

Bessie, who seems to have always exhibited some personality and health problems, married a Lithuanian Jew, Arnold, a butcher who had spent a number of years in a planned but eventually unsuccessful Jewish settlement in Argentina. For their wedding Rebecca organized an outdoor ceremony at the house, cooking the traditional food and creating the festive atmosphere she knew how to do so well. Bessie and Arnold's marriage vows were held under a *chuppah* (a wedding canopy) formed by live tree branches.

Almost immediately after their wedding, things started to go wrong in their relationship. Arnold showed himself as a crude, coarse man. Their marriage was filled with arguments, frequent moves, and endless chaos. The couple was viewed with disdain by Rebecca and the rest of the family. Sometimes Rebecca was sympathetic and offered assistance and concern. Other times she gave up on them, refusing to let them stay in the house, and spouting deep displeasure at their behaviors. Rebecca tried to instill in Bessie the notion of making do, something she regarded as one of her own great strengths. That approach didn't work with Bessie and Arnold. Their fighting and unruly existence didn't change. They never had children. Their fraught and fragile marriage lasted twelve years, until Bessie died at age thirty-eight from a gangrened leg. Rebecca's health had been failing at the same time that Bessie was also on a downward slope. Rebecca died in June 1940. Bessie died on August 1 that same year, but no one told her that her mother had died only two months before.

Minnie in her growing-up years was the rebel in the family. She would slip out of a back window to go to local dances, something that

Rebecca would surely have forbidden. She was a free spirit, occasionally leaving home to stay with a friend of dubious character, talking coyly with sexual innuendo, and branching out from an office job into creating her own antiques business. She bought her own Model A Ford and no one could figure out how she had enough money to do that. Minnie and Rebecca argued a lot. But each time Minnie defied Rebecca by pushing against her strict standards and moving from the house, Minnie would come back and Rebecca took her in with cautious forgiveness. Underneath it all, Rebecca loved her and her joyous nature. In 1931, Minnie met and married Gabriel, a pharmacist, who wanted to own a drug store. Minnie vowed to find money to help him, but she got pregnant soon after marriage. Rebecca eagerly anticipated the birth of her first grandchild, but in yet another tragedy, Minnie developed eclampsia and died in childbirth at age twenty-eight. The child was never born. Minnie's joyful optimism was gone. Rebecca and the entire family mourned for all of their remaining years.

Lena, who stayed at home until after Rebecca's death, married late and never had children, perhaps because she had seen the hazards of childbearing with her mother and sister. She worked all her life in steady secretarial jobs and never created problems. Lena did have a sense of adventure and travelled to Europe in 1940—unwise in retrospect—probably after Rebecca and Bessie had died, and even though World War II had already begun. Her basic personality was positive and rock solid. Rebecca would have been happy with Lena.

Joe married and had two children. He went to work as a salesman, but somehow missed Rebecca's strong influence and message of honest effort. He ended up failing his family. He was a compulsive gambler who embezzled from his employer, and took money that was designated to pay for his daughter's wedding. He died suddenly at fifty-nine, leaving his wife close to destitution and homelessness. If she had lived, Rebecca would have been dismayed by Joe's behavior.

Eddie gained commercial office skills in high school and joined the army on December 7, 1941, the day of the attack on Pearl Harbor. He was not eligible for combat because he wore glasses and was assigned to administrative duties. He was one of the stenographers in the early Nuremberg trials. After his military service in Europe, he married, never had children, and spent his entire life as a court stenographer in the Boston court system. Rebecca would have been proud of him.

In an uncanny way, Rebecca still managed to maintain control over her children, even in their deaths. Rebecca is buried close by her two older daughters. On their gravestones the names are engraved as Bessie Goldberg and Minnie Goldberg, even though they had been married and officially bore their husbands' names.

GRAVE ON LEFT: BESSIE GOLDBERG
GRAVE ON RIGHT: MINNIE GOLDBERG AND
REBECCA GOLDBERG

Rebecca died at age sixty-four. Her cause of death was likely from heart disease, but no record exists. Her obituary was simple and straightforward, and not revealing anything of her fraught life.

MRS. REBECCA GOLDBERG

Mrs. Rebecca Goldberg died [June 2, 1940] at her home on Fairview Avenue Monday night after a long illness. She was 69 [sic] years old and had been a resident of Wilmington the past 30 years. Funeral services were held at the Levine funeral parlors in Dorchester and burial was in Montvale, yesterday afternoon. She leaves three sons, Edward and Joseph of Wilmington, Louie of Providence; two daughters, Lena Goldberg and Mrs. Bessie Gould of Wilmington; a sister, Mrs. Levie of Brookline, and a brother, Morris of Dorchester.

Things may have been different for Rebecca in another era. If she had not been born into poverty and had come to America at an earlier age, she would have gone to school, been one of the top students in her grade, and gone to college. If she had been free of some of the traditional attitudes towards daughters or had the advantage of an education, she may have had a say in whom to marry. With a higher economic status, she may have had better access to birth control information as did women with greater financial means. The time and society she lived in severely limited her options. Still, under these circumstances, she did extraordinarily well and accomplished a great deal for a poor woman of her generation.

Rebecca's life was a mixture of accomplishment and some joy, but littered with tragedy. Her children saw her enjoying herself at times, but she couldn't accept happiness. She believed that sorrow surrounded her and she often stated that she never had a happy day, even though her children saw her seeming to enjoy herself.

She had developed an ever-present wariness about life that started early with her sister, Leah's, and her son, Joey's, premature deaths. She was strong enough to get through the first few years of a desolate marriage, but numerous dreadful occurrences shaped how she reacted to life. Any day could bring bad news. Even though there were many years between heart-breaking events, she knew that misery was out there, ready to land. She waited and expected it to happen, and it did. Rebecca concluded that it was better to harden herself and anticipate disaster than be surprised, unprepared, and lose control as a result.

Rebecca accomplished much of what she set out to do, although she had trouble seeing it. She survived, kept the family together, and maintained a safe place for them all to live. All of her children met or even exceeded her expectations for education, and those who survived went on to self-sufficiency—except for Joe. She did all of this by extraordinary hard physical work and clever strategies, which included breaking the law. She saw herself as being self-sufficient, but realistically, she didn't do this totally alone. She relied on family, friends, and her children to get through. She was the embodiment of strength. People were drawn to her and willing to help support her because she proved herself through the art of every-day survival.

AFTERWORD

Everyone who knew Rebecca has died, including all of her children. Her five grandchildren were either too young to remember her or had not been born before she died. Only a few photographs, newspaper articles, and the words of her sons and daughter have survived her. Except for the house on Fairview Avenue, no physical evidence of her life remains. Interestingly, the public records for the house indicate that it was built in 1920. This was the year that Rebecca most likely had the money to complete the roof. There are no personal possessions, no writings, and no bottles of blueberry wine. It is 130 years since

Rebecca stepped off the boat onto American soil, and 2020 marks the eightieth anniversary of her death. Her husband, Nathan, died a little more than one hundred years ago. This all seems like such a long time ago, but her life's struggle is not an old story. It is real and still repeated in the lives of current-day poor immigrants whose primary goals are to make enough money to survive and to keep their families together.

Many details of Rebecca's life are obscure, but enough of her legacy has remained to be passed on not only to her descendants, but to many who want to know and appreciate one woman's determination and single-mindedness. Her story demonstrates powerfully not only what it takes to endure, but what is required to establish hope and a foothold for future generations.

ᴀCKNOWLEDGMENTS

This quite small book is the result of what feels like a gigantic amount of work. For more than five years, I searched for information about my grandmother, my family, and the eras in which they lived. I was confronted with puzzling questions at each stage of the process and strove to find answers. I faced conundrums such as clarifying my goals for the project; what voice I wanted to use in presenting the story; what information to gather and what to accept or reject for inclusion; what messages I wanted readers to come away with; and how to tell the tale in the most accurate and respectful way possible.

I received invaluable help, advice, and input from a number of people who contributed to the final product.

David O'Neil, my trusted long-term mentor, gave me questions to think about and told me to write down my responses and reflect on them in order to clarify my purpose. Laurel Kayne, my exceptional editor, read and reread the manuscript and doggedly pointed out where statements I made in one section didn't jibe with other sections, or showed me when I had already said the same thing two or three times.

During an extended period of research, Shulamith Berger, Curator of Special Collections and Hebraica-Judaica, Mendel Gottesman Library, Yeshiva University, retrieved and provided me with documents from the *Peter Wiernik and Bertha Wiernik Collection – 1886–1950* at their research center in New York City. Staff and clergy at the Jewish Cemetery Association of Massachusetts helped me understand burial practices, especially for women, in the late nineteenth and early twentieth centuries.

If it weren't for Alesia Maltz, one of my primary faculty advisors at the Antioch University New England, Environmental Studies Department, I would never have known that I could be a writer. In one of my classes with her, I read an essay I had written about my father's family, the Goldbergs. "You should have that published," she said. That one comment sent me on a journey of writing and publication that I could never have imagined for myself. My original essay was published in Antioch's 2003-2004 edition of the literary journal, *Whole Terrain*, as *The Resilience of Memory* and under the author name of Leah Majofis. Alesia's words changed my life.

Another of my faculty advisors, Heidi Watts, provided me with a model of how to live a diverse, purposeful, and innovative existence. Heidi has divided her life among numerous locations, including New Hampshire, Nova Scotia, and India. In each of these places she contributes to her communities, inspires people, and is creative through her writings.

Family members also provided their memories and personal research about the Goldbergs and Wernicks. Sidney Stillerman Royer helped unveil the mystery of Leah Wernick's tragic early death and where she was buried. My brother, Arthur Gilbert, and sister, Paula Gilbert, both contributed their recollections about Goldberg and Wernick family members. Previously unknown (at least to me) knowledge about the Majofis family came from Itzhak Pomerantz in Israel and Arie Band in Switzerland. My connection to them happened because of my Antioch article published under the name of Leah Majofis.

Friend and coauthor on a previous book Vivien Goldman graciously provided the photo of me that appears in the book. Friend and neighbor Rita Sullivan listened to my endless updates on the book's progress as I worked toward getting it to press.

My children and grandchildren—Philip Knapp, Vickie Jackson, Hannah and Samuel Jackson Knapp, Daniel Knapp, Mari Hirono, and Lina Hirono Knapp, all of whom I love deeply—were constant incentives as they gently bugged me about when the book would be available for them to read.

The fine members of my She Writes Press team—Lauren Wise, Shannon Green, and Brooke Warner—challenged me to think clearly and kept me on track and on schedule. Tabitha Lahr provided an incredible cover and the beautiful interior design of the book.

My greatest motivation for writing this book came from the people who are no longer living. The powerful memories of my father, Louis Gilbert, my aunt Lena Goldberg Bobrow, and my uncle Edward Goldberg provided persistent exhortations to tell this story of tough challenges and enduring spirit.

SELECTED TITLES FROM SHE WRITES PRESS

She Writes Press is an independent publishing
company founded to serve women writers everywhere.
Visit us at www.shewritespress.com.

Dearest Ones at Home: Clara Taylor's Letters from Russia,
1917-1919 edited by Katrina Maloney and Patricia Maloney.
$18.95, 978-1-63152-931-3. Clara Taylor's detailed, delightful
letters documenting her two years in Russia teaching factory
girls self-sufficiency skills—right in the middle of World War I.

When a Toy Dog Became a Wolf and the Moon Broke Curfew:
A Memoir by Hendrika de Vries. $16.95, 978-1631526589.
Hendrika is "Daddy's little girl," but when Nazis occupy
Amsterdam and her father is deported to a POW labor camp,
she must bond with her mother—who joins the Resistance after
her husband's deportation—and learn about female strength in
order to discover the strong woman she can become.

The Beauty of What Remains: Family Lost, Family Found
by Susan Johnson Hadler. $16.95, 978-1-63152-007-5. Susan
Johnson Hadler goes on a quest to find out who the missing
people in her family were—and what happened to them—and
succeeds in reuniting a family shattered for four generations.

Surviving the Survivors: A Memoir by Ruth Klein. $16.95,
978-1-63152-471-4. With both humor and deep feeling, Klein
shares the story of her parents—who survived the Holocaust
but could not overcome the tragedy they had experienced—
and their children, who became indirect victims of the
atrocities endured by the generation before them.

Veronica's Grave: A Daughter's Memoir by Barbara Bracht
Donsky. $16.95, 978-1-63152-074-7. A loss and coming-of-
age story that follows young Barbara Bracht as she struggles
to comprehend the sudden disappearance and death of her
mother and cope with a blue-collar father intent upon erasing
her mother's memory.